Usborne
Sticker Dolly Dressing
Action! & Ice Skaters

Action!

Illustrated by Steven Wood

Written by Fiona Watt   Designed by Non Figg

Contents:

Air ambulance crew

The dolls pull on their flying gear as soon as they arrive at the helipad so they're prepared to zoom off for any emergency they might have to attend. It could be someone seriously hurt in a traffic accident, a walker who's fallen on a mountainside or perhaps someone thrown from a horse.

Lexie

Ella

Kate

Snowboarding

Gemma, Millie and Beth are snowboarding champions. It was snowing heavily when they climbed into bed last night, but they woke to find perfect conditions. The snow is soft and powdery, so their boards carve deep tracks as they zoom down the mountain.

Gemma

Beth
Millie

Emergency!

As firefighters, Lola, Izzy and Georgie are used to coping with emergencies. When the alarm sounds, they pull on their protective clothes and race to the scene. They might find themselves tackling a blaze, rescuing someone who's trapped or helping at an accident.

Lola

Izzy
Georgie
7

Filming wildlife

From rainforests in South America to game parks in Africa, the dolls have filmed animals in locations all over the world. At the moment they are filming lemurs on Madagascar, an island in the Indian Ocean.

Gemma

Triathletes

After completing the swimming section of the triathlon, the dolls have rushed onto the shore to get into their cycling gear for the next part of the race. Emma is ready to jump onto her bike and pedal away. The final running stage of the race will be the hardest for them, as they will be getting very tired by then.

Emma

Tracking a suspect

Alyssa and her police dog Ollie are always on the move. They might be tracking a suspect, on the hunt for stolen property or searching for a missing person. If Ollie picks up a scent and finds something, he will sit down and bark.

Special investigations

Lucy is working undercover. She's spent hours trailing a criminal gang to collect evidence about their activities and whereabouts. Later today, she'll report back to the detectives in charge of the case.

Lucy

On the stage

"Starting positions everyone please..."
Erin, Asha and Becky are rehearsing for
a new musical which opens in two weeks.
Each performance will be over two and a
half hours long, and they'll be doing eight
shows a week. It will be exhausting but
the dolls are excited about wowing the
audience with their amazing routines
and dazzling costumes.

Erin

Asha
Becky

Sub-zero temperatures

Holly, Nicole and Ellie are three scientists living in Antarctica for a few months. When they venture away from the research station they need to wrap up in lots of layers to protect them from the freezing polar winds. When the dolls aren't working they go exploring on skidoos or trudge across the ice on skis to take photos of the spectacular landscape.

Holly

Ellie

Nicole

Movie stars

"Lights... camera... ACTION!" The dolls are doing their own stunts in an action-packed adventure movie. They've been chased along busy streets, escaped from burning buildings and jumped from great heights (while wearing safety harnesses, of course).

BG12 RR4
Libby
Kirsten

Riding competition

The dolls are competing in a three-day riding competition. Yesterday they took part in the dressage event where they rode their horses calmly through a series of trots, canters and turns. Today has been more energetic as they've jumped the huge fences and obstacles in the cross-country. Tomorrow it's showjumping.

Amelie
Amy

Jetting away

Millionaires, movie stars, celebrities and even royalty have flown with the dolls, who are the crew of a luxury private jet. They've pampered their passengers on flights all around the world - on trips to exclusive ski resorts, privately-owned tropical islands and secluded chic hotels.

Natalie

Megan
Paige

Inshore rescue

Carla, Lottie and Anya are part of a team that rescue people who get into difficulties near the coast. They've plucked people from rocks who've been cut off by the tide, helped boats stranded on sandbanks and even rescued a cow stuck on a muddy riverbank.

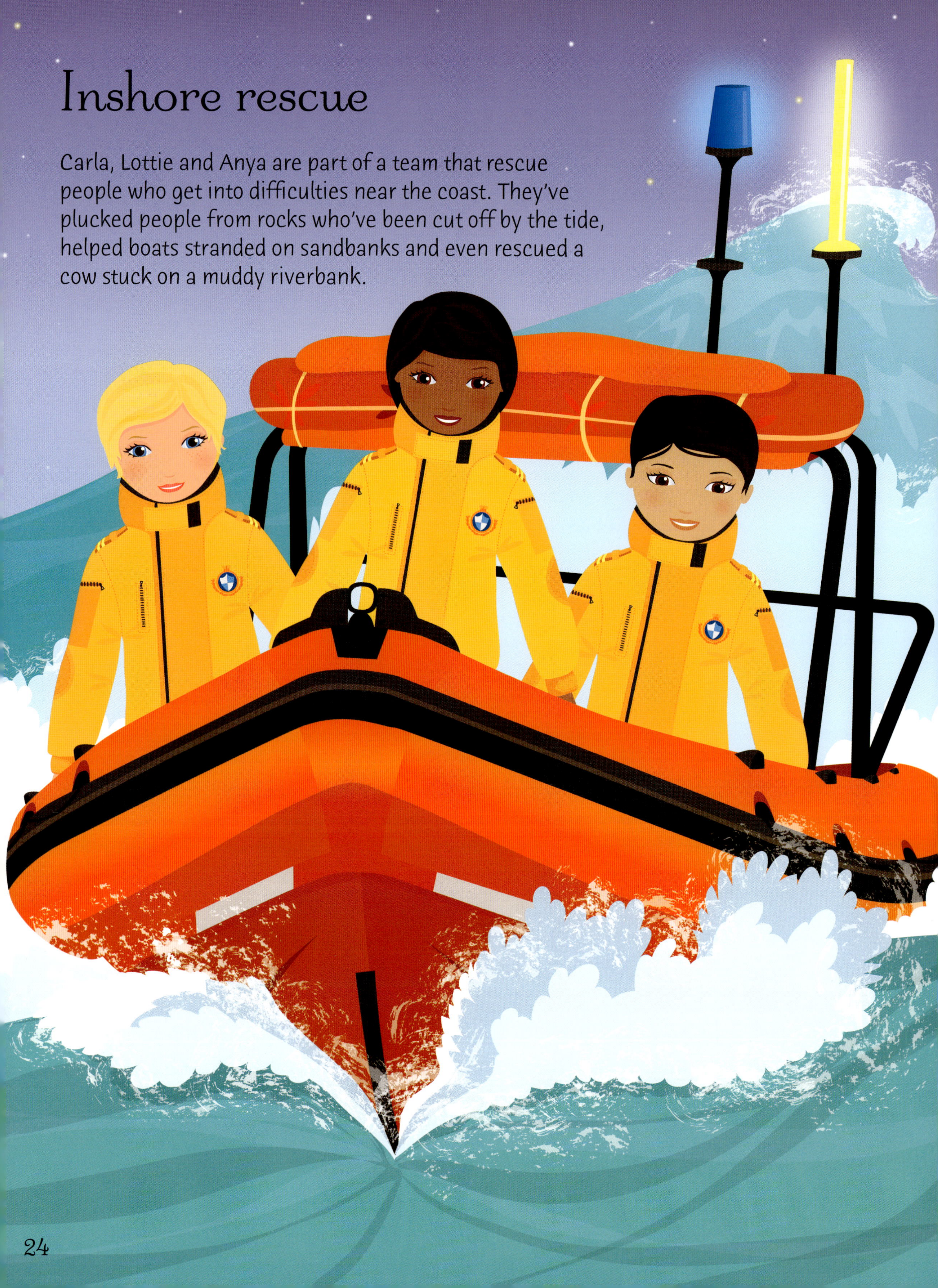

Air ambulance crew
The stickers fit on all the dolls.
Pages 2-3

Snowboarding
The stickers fit on all the dolls.
Pages 4-5

Emergency!
The stickers fit on all the dolls.
Dials for the fire truck
Pages 6-7

Filming wildlife

The stickers fit on all
the dolls.

Triathletes
Emma's helmet
31
Tilly's swimming hat
Tilly's wetsuit, worn on top of her running suit
31
The running suits fit on all the dolls.
33
32
Pages 10-11
Tracking a suspect
013
Page 12
Alyssa's belt

Special investigations
Page 13
On the stage
The stickers fit
on all the dolls.
Pages 14-15

Sub-zero temperatures
The stickers fit on all the dolls.
Put the neck warmers on before the jackets.
Pages 16-17

Movie stars
Chloë's socks
Chloë's outfit
Chloë's boots
Kirsten's microphone
Kirsten's socks
Kirsten's gloves
Kirsten's watch
Libby's watch
Libby's socks
Libby's clothes and boots
Libby's safety harness
Lighting for the crash mat
Pages 18–19

Riding competition
The stickers fit
on all the dolls.
Medical armbands
Put the body protectors
on top of the shirts.
Pages 20-21

Jetting away
The stickers fit on all the dolls.
Pages 22-23
Inshore rescue
Put the helmets on before the buoyancy aids.
Page 24

Usborne
Sticker Dolly Dressing
Ice Skaters

Designed and illustrated by Stella Baggott

Written by Fiona Watt

Contents

At the ice rink

Natalie, Ellie and Jess are best friends who love to skate. They often meet up and spend the afternoon skating on an ice rink in the park.

Ellie adores fashion and loves choosing her glittery outfits that she wears for skating competitions.
PARK CAFÉ
Jess loves taking part in skating competitions. She goes over and over her steps, jumps and spins until they are perfect.

Buying new skates

The dolls are out shopping, looking for new skates as their old ones are battered and scuffed. Ellie's spotted some bright pink skates that she thinks might match her new competition outfit.

A training session

Twice a week, Jess, Ellie and Natalie have skating
lessons together. Their coach teaches them new steps
and turns, and builds their confidence on the ice, too.

In the gym

The dolls spend time in the gym at the rink, where they do exercises to make their bodies strong and flexible. They also do ballet exercises too, to help them look graceful during their ice dance routines.

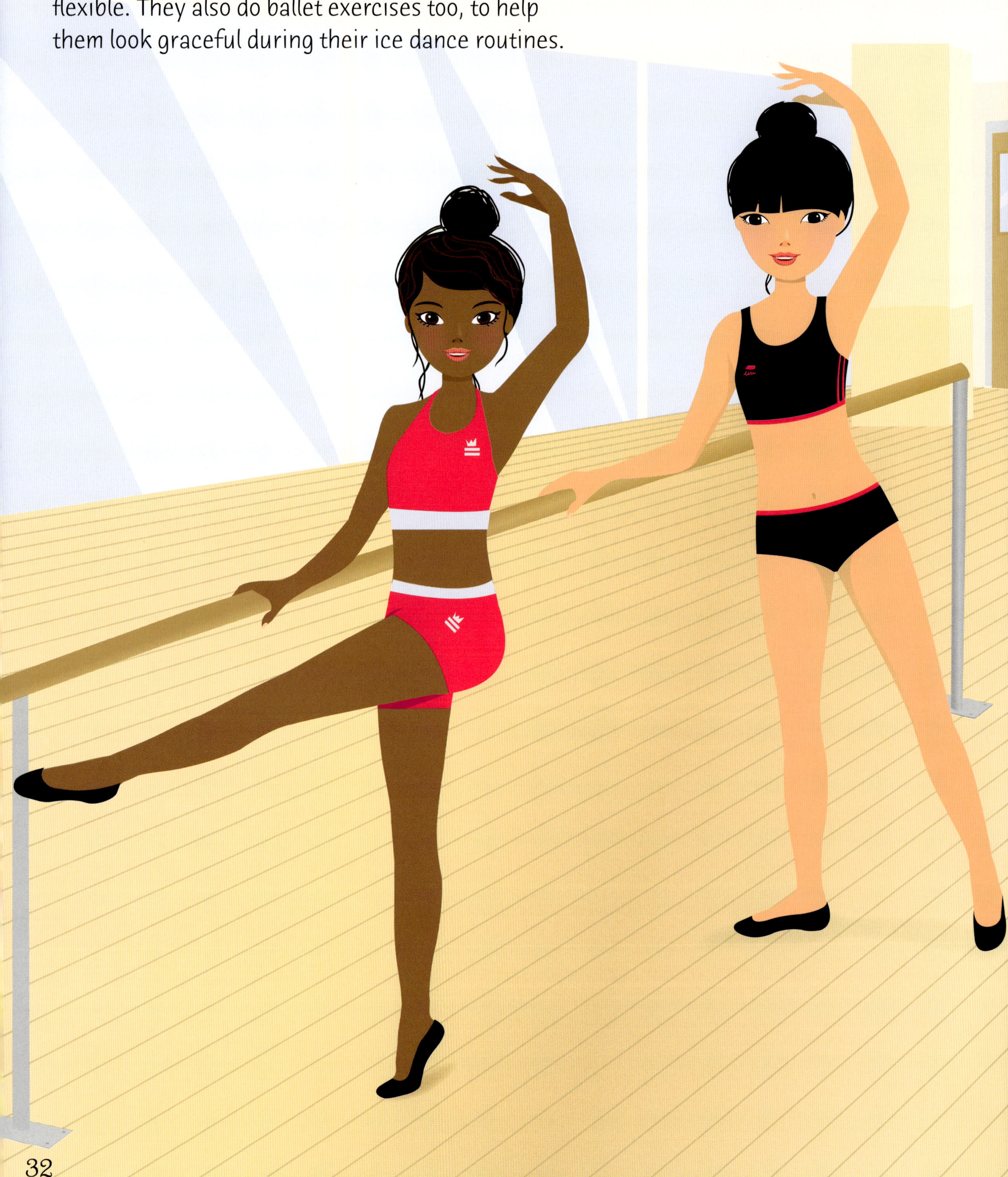

Costume fitting

The dolls are taking part in a figure skating competition and they need new outfits for their ice dance routines. Ellie and Natalie really love the sparkling beads and sequins on their dresses.

Jess's dream

Jess hopes that one day she'll
be good enough to have a
skating partner. They would do
complicated spins and lifts as they
glided gracefully around the ice.

Twisting lift

Jess dreams that she'll also be able to
do a move known as a twist lift. Her
skating partner would lift her into the
air and she would twist around and
around, before he caught her.

Ballet on ice

Natalie, Jess and Ellie have come to watch
a performance of Swan Lake on ice. They
are enchanted by the breathtaking skill
of the skaters, the amazing costumes
and the beautiful music.

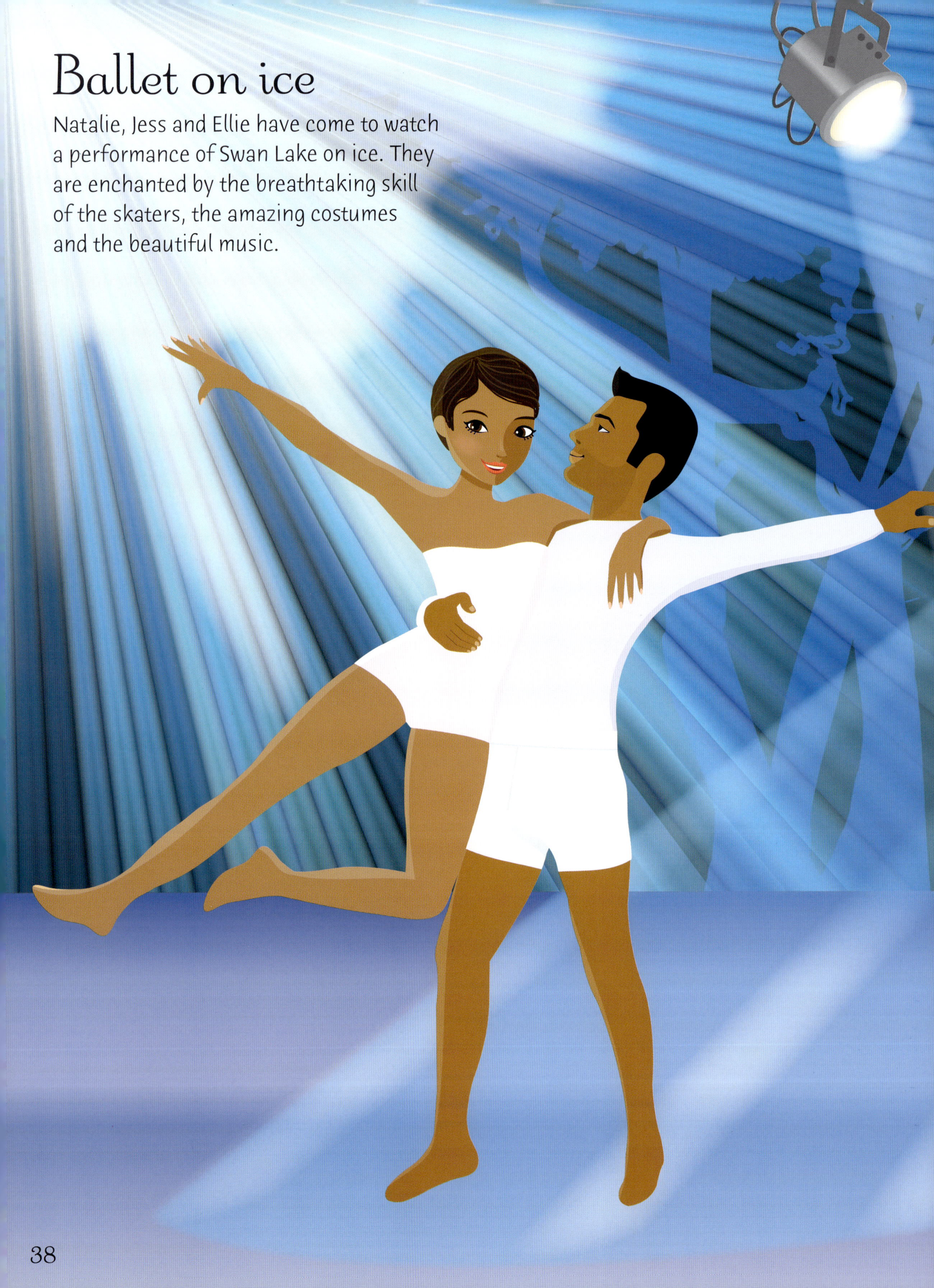

Ice show

The dolls would love to skate in a circus on ice.
They would wear dazzling costumes that would
sparkle and shimmer under the spotlights. Natalie
could do lots of acrobatic leaps and jumps, and
Ellie might fly up from the ice on a trapeze.

Skating in the snow

It's Ellie's birthday and the dolls have arranged
a skating party at an outdoor rink. They show
off their skating skills in the middle of the
rink, as the snow gently falls around them.

CAFÉ

Ice hockey

Natalie loves the thrill of a fast-paced ice hockey match. She enjoys hearing the supporters' roar as she chases the rubber puck. Her chunky skates allow her to make rapid stops and turns as she zooms across the ice.

Speed skating

When Natalie isn't figure skating, training or
playing ice hockey, she's often at the speed
skating rink. She enjoys the speed at which
the skaters race around the oval ice track.

Celebrity competition

The dolls are in the studio audience of
a television skating competition. They
would love to be taking part, dressed
up in the amazing outfits and trying to
impress the panel of judges.

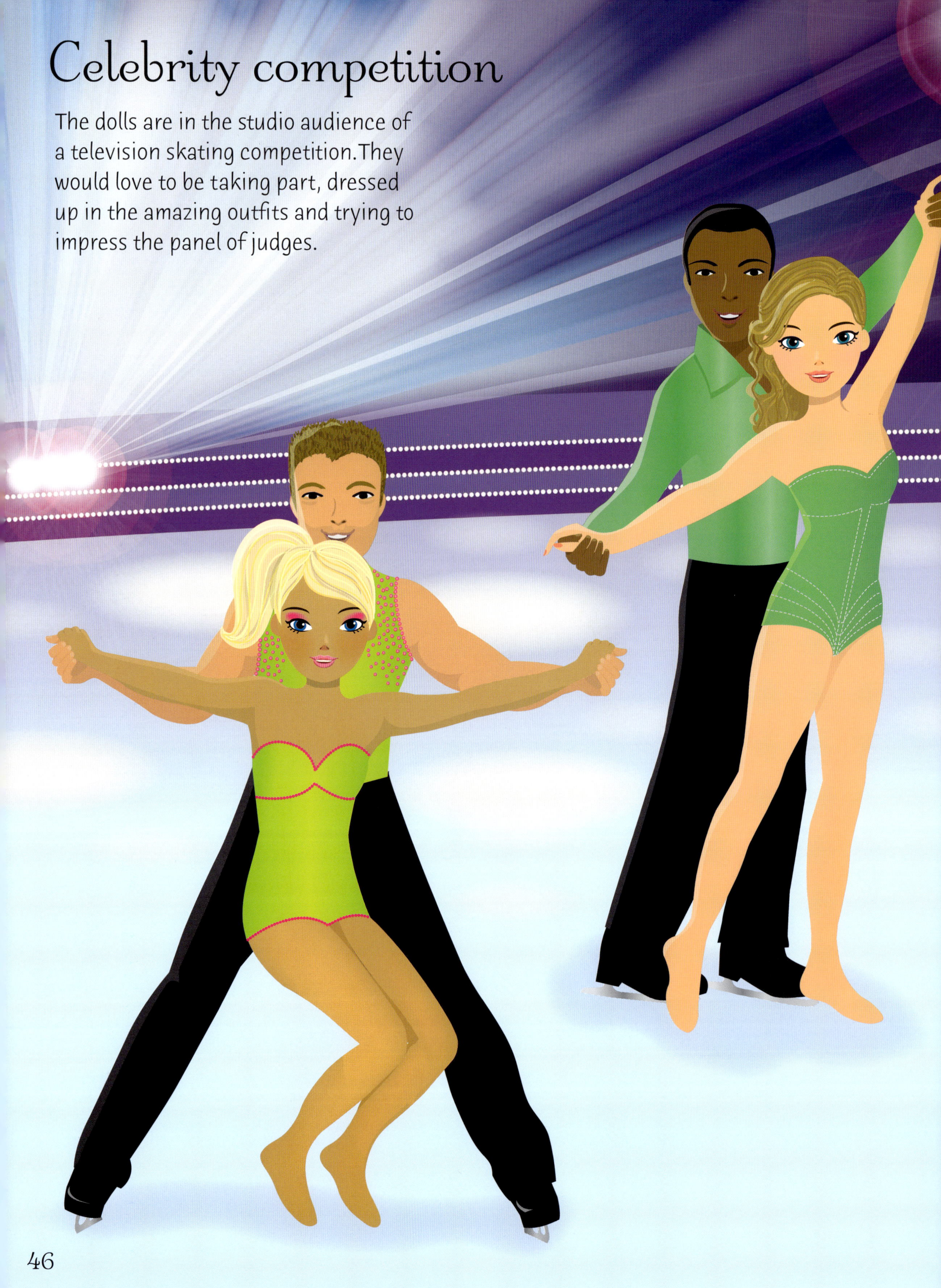

8
8
7
47

Medal ceremony

"And the winner of the gold medal is ......"
The dolls are dreaming that they're standing
on the podium with medals hanging around
their necks. Maybe they will, one day?

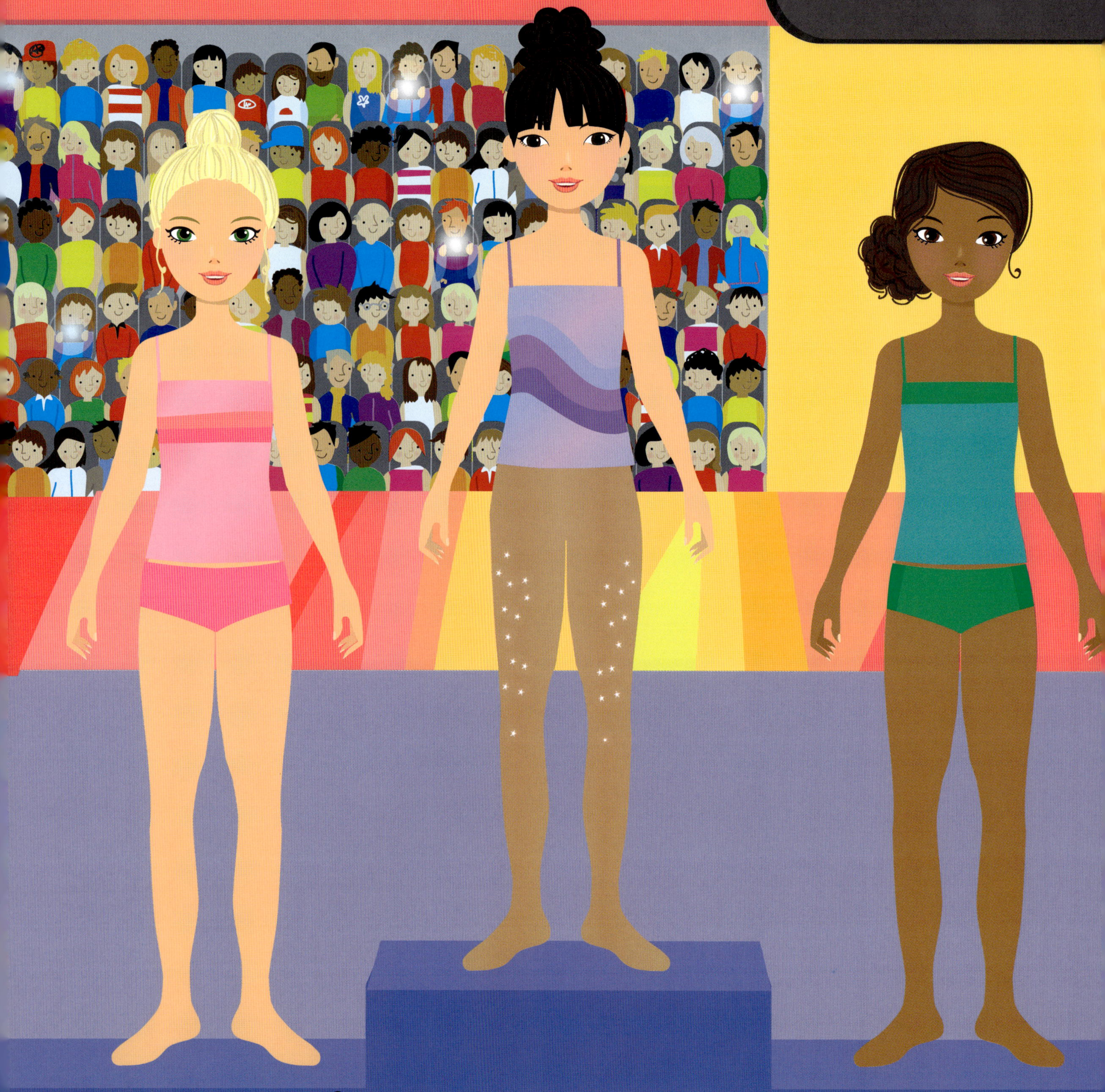

Buying new skates pages 28-29
Put the leggings and socks on Ellie, first.
Ellie's dress
Ellie's skates
Ellie's skates
Skates for the display shelves

A training session pages 30-31
Follow the numbers in purple to dress Natalie.
Her sleeve
1
2
3
4
5
Her body warmer
Put on Jess's tights, then her skirt and then her skates.
Gloves
Jess's legwarmers go over her skates.
Follow the numbers in blue to dress Ellie.
1
2
3
4
5
Skates
6
Skates
6
7
Natalie's gloves
Skates

In the gym pages 32-33
Jess's leggings
Jess's sweatshirt
Jess's shorts, top and legwarmers
Sweatbands
Put Natalie's shorts on before her skirt.
Put this over the purple top.
A headband
Ellie's leggings
Ellie's top and shorts
Hand weights

Costume fitting pages 34-35
The stickers fit all of the dolls.
Rolls of material
'Sleeves' for the turquoise dress
Add these sketches to the board.
Put the sewing equipment on the table and shelves.

Jess's dream page 36
The tights go over the skates.
Twisting lift page 37
The tights go over the skates.

Ballet on ice pages 38-39
Put this sticker on first.
Dress the man before the ballerina.
The White Swan's outfit
Arm sleeve
The Black Swan's outfit
A spotlight

Ice show pages 40-41
Add the tights first, then the wings and bodice.
Natalie's outfit is green and turquoise.
Jess's costume is orange.
Ellie's clothes are pink.

Skating in the snow pages 42-43
Ellie's tights and shorts
Ellie's sweater
Ellie's poncho
Legwarmers go over the skates.
Jess's tights and skirt
Jess's jacket and skates
Natalie's skirt and jacket
Natalie's gloves
Put on Natalie's leggings, then her socks.
Natalie's skates

Ice hockey page 44
Follow the numbers to dress Natalie.
1
2
Body protectors
3
Footless socks
4
5
6
7
8
Ice hockey stick
9
Speed skating page 45
Follow the numbers. The outfits are in the order they appear on the page.
1
1
1
Bodysuit
2
2
2
3
3
3
4
4
4
5
5
5
6
6
6
7
7
7
Helmet

Celebrity competition pages 46-47
Match the clothes to their partners'.
Medal ceremony page 48
These stickers fit all the dolls.